Speak the Truth in Love: Learning to Discuss Your Faith in Chinese

by C.K.

Copyright © 2012 by C.K.

ISBN-13:
978-1481188210

ISBN-10:
1481188216

Contents:

Acknowledgements	vii
How to Use This Book	xi
Part I	
Lesson 1: God's Existence	16
Lesson 2: God's Character	18
Lesson 3: Humanity's Problem	20
Lesson 4: God Solves this Problem	22
Lesson 5: Your Decision	24
Lesson 6: The Bible	26
Lesson 7: Prayer	28
Lesson 8: Prosperous Life	30
Lesson 9: God Transcends Culture	32
Lesson 10: Chinese Christians	34
Lesson 11: Atheism is a Kind of Faith	36
Part II	
Lesson 12: "Nobody can prove God exists…"	40
Lesson 13: "What is God? What is He like?"	44
Lesson 14: Humanity's Problem	48
Lesson 15: "Who can solve this problem?"	52
Lesson 16: Your Decision	58
Lesson 17: "My life goal is to earn money…"	62
Lesson 18: "All Americans are Christians, right?"	66
Lesson 19: "… I just believe in myself."	70
Lesson 20: "What is the Bible?"	72
Lesson 21: "Christianity vs. Chinese culture?"	76
Lesson 22: "Does Christianity conflict with science?"	80
Lesson 23: "Where did this universe come from?"	84
Lesson 24: "Is Christianity a Western religion?"	88
Lesson 25: "How is Christianity different…"	90
Lesson 26: "If I have a relationship with God…"	92
Glossary	96

Acknowledgements:

I want to thank everyone who helped me work on this book. M, DC, and J were particularly helpful, spending significant time looking over the Chinese text and explaining their suggestions and changes. They were friendly and encouraging, but also gently critical. This book would have been pretty ugly without them. I also want to acknowledge Delane. She was fantastic to work with and did an incredible job.

Jens and Vinny, two of my closest friends during the writing season, were incredibly encouraging to me while I wrote this. They consistently went above and beyond the call of duty to be friends with me, invite me into their lives, and encourage me. It would have been difficult to stay sane this past year without them.

John, Michael, Smange, Chris, and Jordan, five dear friends from East Asia, have modeled to me over the past few years how to be a friend. They have poured into me significantly, and have shaped my character profoundly. Words simply cannot express my gratitude to God for putting them in my life.

Chris, Kristin, and Shannon kept me alive while I was in Asia learning Chinese. They cared for me, let me be myself, and faithfully encouraged me whenever I was discouraged (which was often — without them I might have stopped trying to learn Chinese altogether). I will never forget late nights out at the bar, attempting to watch videos on the crummy internet at their house, or simply complaining about how cold we all were in the winter. Their company was sweet and irreplaceable.

Patrick got me started writing a book in the first place. He thinks he can do literally anything, and goes about life with such confidence that he ends up being able to do pretty much whatever he sets out to do. This attitude has had a huge effect on me. I probably wouldn't have tried to write a book if it weren't for seeing him accomplish so many things I thought impossible.

All the Chinese Christians I have met, both in America and abroad, have been nothing but kind and welcoming to me. Not only that, but God has particularly used relationships with several Chinese Christians to teach me through example what courage, sacrifice, wisdom, and a spirit of unity can mean. For their safety, I am hesitant to name them in this book, but they have nonetheless meant a great deal to me.

Finally I want to acknowledge my parents. They have always believed in me, and have never rolled their eyes at anything I've set out to do. They suffered separation from me for several years without flinching or pressuring me. More than anything, they've taught me what it means to love another person. I look at the way they treat each other, and how they treat me, and I see what love means.

How to Use this Book

Maybe the best way to introduce this book is to explain what it is not. This is not a systematic textbook. By the time you finish going through this book, you will not be able to "get around" in China, and there will be very basic grammar and vocabulary you will not have been exposed to here.

This book is simply meant to give you the tools you need to clearly discuss your faith in Chinese. You will learn words like "resurrect," "worldview," and "grace," but not "cat," "dog," or "library." The language in these lessons is not elegant Chinese, nor is it necessarily how a native Chinese-speaker would address these topics. You can think of it as being a little like baby-talk. It teaches how to explain yourself clearly and correctly, but you will probably still sound foreign.

The theory behind this approach is simple. When you are learning a new language, progress is slow. Acquiring new vocabulary is painstaking, and you typically have a vastly oversimplified understanding of the language's grammar. But you probably have a limited time serving in a Chinese-speaking population. You want to be able to discuss your faith soon, without having to wade through the years of study that would normally be necessary to talk about something as complex as faith.

That is where this book comes in. Its goal is to give you a very small set of tools and teach you to use them in a way that maximizes your ability to share, at the cost of elegance. I once lived with a guy who worked on cars a lot, and he was fond of saying "If I have duct tape, a wrench, and WD-40 I can fix anything. It won't be pretty but it'll work." The purpose of this book is to give you the linguistic equivalents of duct tape, a wrench, and WD-40 — and then teach you to use them.

Part I assumes no prior knowledge of Chinese except for familiarity with the pinyin system of pronunciation. (If you need to learn it, just poke around on the internet. It's pretty simple, but beyond the scope of this book to explain). After completing the first five lessons, you will be able to succinctly explain the Gospel. The next six lessons will teach you how to express simple summaries of what Christians believe about a variety of topics that commonly come up in conversation with Chinese people.

Part II is more intermediate-level. Almost all of the lessons are based on questions Chinese non-Christians often ask. It begins with a more in-depth Gospel presentation, and moves to topics such as conflict between science and faith, the ways a person's life changes upon trusting Christ, and the difference between "believing in oneself" and religious faith.

There are 26 lessons total in this book. Everyone learns at

her own pace, but depending on your schedule, you might think about averaging a lesson every two weeks to get through the book in a year, or one lesson a week to get through it in two school semesters.

I'm not including any exercises or tests because everyone has different language-learning goals. Some people really want to learn to read and write; others couldn't care less. Some will already have a solid Chinese foundation and are just looking for spiritual vocabulary; others have never studied before and need a thorough walk-through. Each lesson is simply a Chinese passage, followed by vocabulary used in the passage, and a direct translation into English of the passage. (Note: this is a direct translation from the Chinese, so the language will sound stilted). Here are three ways you can use this format to test yourself depending on what you want to accomplish:

- Memorize each lesson. Once you are able to recite a lesson from memory, move on to the next one.

- Cover up the character and definition in the vocabulary list for each lesson. Looking only at the pinyin (pronunciation), try to recall the definition and/or write the character. Do the same for the English and the Chinese characters.

- Take each word in a vocabulary list and try to use it in a sentence. Get a native-speaker to check your sentences to see if they are grammatically and syntactically correct.

A few final thoughts:

Textbooks tend to be great at teaching people to speak, read, and write, but not as good at teaching people to listen. As you work through these lessons, take special time not just to memorize vocabulary and recite sentences, but to listen to the words. Hear how they sound when pronounced correctly. You want to be able to recognize these words when a

Chinese person says them in conversation, in addition to being able to use them in conversation yourself.

Most of my experience has been with young, educated, Han Chinese people. They are wildly different from older, rural, poor, uneducated, or minority people. If you are serving in any of these other populations, this book will definitely still be helpful, but you will need to pay close attention to the types of questions these people ask, and the issues they care most about. Don't work really hard on the lessons on science vs. faith or the origin of the universe if you are in a population that doesn't care about science.

This book is meant for a Christian language-learner. You will be disappointed if you treat it like a systematic apologetic treatise or a guide to winning arguments with non-Christians. I'm neither a theologian nor rhetorician. I'm just trying to give a simple way to tell people what you believe and answer some of the questions they might have about it.

When you finish this book — or even before you finish — a fantastic resource is the Good News Reader, published by Happy Hour Publishing. It's more advanced and will take your spiritual language to the next level. It's been around for a long time, and I highly recommend it. You can find it here:

http://www.afcresources.org/bookstore/contents/en-us/d140.html#p30892

第一部分
Part One

第一课：神的存在

对很多人来说神是不存在的，但是神真的存在。神不但存在，而且神创造了宇宙，创造了你和我。他也爱我们。

dì yī	第一	first
kè	课	lesson
shénde	神的	God's
shén	神	God
de	的	[possessive, equivalent to 's in English]
cúnzài	存在	existence, to exist
duì...lái shuō	对...来说	according to...
hěn duō	很多	many
rén	人	people, person
shì...de	是[adjective]的	to be [adjective]
shì	是	to be, is
de	的	[indicates the preceding word is an adjective]
bù	不	[negates whatever follows it]
dànshì	但是	but
zhēn de	真的	really, actually
bùdàn...érqiě	不但...而且	not only...but also
chuàngzào	创造	to create

everyday words

le	了	[used after a verb to indicate the action has already happened]
yǔzhòu	宇宙	universe
nǐ	你	you
hé	和	and
wǒ	我	me, I
tā	他	he
yě	也	also
ài	爱	to love
wǒmen	我们	we, us
men	们	[used to indicate more than one person]

世界 Shì jiè

Translation:

Lesson 1: God's Existence

According to a lot of people, God does not exist. But He actually does exist. God not only exists, but He also created the universe. He created you and me. He also loves us.

[Note: as I said in the "How to Use this Book" section, these are direct translations from the Chinese, so the English will sound a bit stilted and unnatural.]

第二课：神的品格

神是完美的，伟大的。神没有任何的罪恶和缺点。神完全了解每个人，神想跟每个人建立关系。

dì èr	第二	second
pǐngé	品格	character
wánměi	完美	perfect
wěidà	伟大	great, mighty
méi	没	[negates whatever follows it]
yǒu	有	to have
rènhé	任何	any
zuì'è	罪恶	sin
hé	和	and, with [because of the use of "any," 和 translates to "or" in this sentence, but technically means "and"]
quēdiǎn	缺点	shortcoming
wánquán	完全	completely
liǎojiě	了解	to understand [implies deep, comprehensive understanding]
měi	每	every
gè	个	[generic measure word]
xiǎng	想	to want

gēn	跟	with
jiànlì	建立	to establish
guānxì	关系	relationship

Translation:

Lesson 2: God's Character

God is perfect and mighty. God does not have any sin or shortcoming. God completely understands every person. God wants to have a relationship with every person.

第三课：人类的问题

但是我们不是完美的。我们往往会做不好的事，会有邪恶的态度，或者拒绝做好的行为。这些不好的事情都叫"罪。"因为我们都有罪，所以我们并不能跟完美的神建立关系。

dìsān	第三	third
rénlèi	人类	humanity, human being
wèntí	问题	problem
wǎngwǎng	往往	often
huì	会	will
zuò	做	to do
bù hǎo	不好	bad
hǎo	好	good
shì	事	stuff, things [abstract, not physical]
xié'è	邪恶	evil
tàidù	态度	attitude
huòzhě	或者	or
jùjué	拒绝	to refuse
xíngwéi	行为	actions, behaviors
zhèxiē	这些	these
shìqíng	事情	same as 事

dōu	都	all
jiào	叫	to be called, to be named
zuì	罪	sin
yīn wéi ... suǒ yǐ	因为...所以	because...so [when translating into English, the "so" is omitted]
bìng	并	[intensifies a negation — so 并不是 is simply a more emphatic way of saying 不是]
néng	能	to be able to

Translation:

Lesson 3: Humanity's Problem

But we are not perfect. We often will do bad things, have evil attitudes, or refuse to do good actions. These bad things are all called "sin." Because we all have sin, we cannot have a relationship with a perfect God.

第四课：神解决问题
dì sì kè: shén jiějué wèntí

但是神的儿子，耶稣基督，离开天堂来到世界上，替我们付了罪的代价。罪的代价是死亡，但是耶稣为我们牺牲他的生命，赎清了我们的罪，给了我们新的生命。

dì sì	第四	fourth
jiějué	解决	to solve
wèntí	问题	problem
érzǐ	儿子	son
yēsū	耶稣	Jesus
jīdū	基督	Christ
líkāi	离开	to leave
tiāntáng	天堂	heaven
lái dào	来到	to come to
shìjiè shàng	世界上	on the earth
shìjiè	世界	the earth, the world
tì...fù	替...付	to pay for [literally "for...to pay"]
zuì	罪	sin
dàijià	代价	price
sǐwáng	死亡	death
wéi	为	for
xīshēng	牺牲	to sacrifice
shēngmìng	生命	life

shúqīng	赎清	to atone for, to redeem
gěi	给	to give
xīn	新	new

Translation:

Lesson 4: God Solves the Problem

But God's son, Jesus Christ, left heaven and came to earth to pay the price for our sins. Sin's price is death, but Jesus sacrificed his life for us, atoned for our sins, and gave us new life.

第五课：你的决定

如果你想经历这样的新生命，你就需要相信耶稣基督真的赎清了你的罪，告诉他你愿意接受这个新生命，并清楚地明白在这个新生命里你不想"走自己的路，"而是想跟随神，走他赐给你的路。

pinyin	汉字	English
dì wǔ	第五	fifth
juédìng	决定	decision
rúguǒ	如果	if
jīnglì	经历	experience
zhèyàng de	这样的	this [literally "this kind of"]
jiù	就	just
xūyào	需要	to need to
xiāngxìn	相信	to believe, to have faith in
gàosù	告诉	to tell
yuànyì	愿意	to be willing to
jiēshòu	接受	to accept, to receive, to take
zhège	这个	this
bìng	并	and, simultaneously [note: here its meaning differs from in Lesson 3]
qīngchǔ de	清楚地	clearly
qīngchǔ	清楚	clear

de	地	[used to indicate the preceding word is an adverb]
míngbái	明白	to understand
zài...lǐ	在...里	in
zǒu zìjǐ de lù	走自己的路	"to walk one's own road"
zǒu	走	to walk
zìjǐ	自己	by oneself
lù	路	road
érshì	而是	but rather
gēnsuí	跟随	to follow
cì gěi	赐给	to give, to bestow upon [or "to give by means of bestowing"]
cì	赐	to bestow
gěi	给	to give

Translation:

Lesson 5: Your Decision

If you want to experience this new life, you must believe that Jesus Christ really atoned for your sin, you must take this new life, and you must clearly understand that in this new life you do not want to "walk your own road," but instead you want to follow God, walking the road He gives you.

第六课：圣经
dì liù kè   shèng jīng

圣经是一封神写给人类的信，是神启示给一些人然后这些人用笔记录下来的话语。所以圣经是人遵照神的意志写下的和谐统一的神的话语。

dì liù	第六	sixth
shèngjīng	圣经	the Bible
yī fēng xìn	一封信	a letter
fēng	封	[measure word for letters]
xìn	信	letter
xiě gěi	写给	to write to [you can think of it as meaning "to give to by means of writing"]
xiě	写	to write
qǐshì gěi	启示给	to reveal to [or "to give to by means of revelation"]
qǐshì	启示	revelation
yīxiē	一些	a few
ránhòu	然后	after
zhèxiē	这些	these
yòng	用	to use
bǐ	笔	pen

jìlù	记录	to record
xiàlái	下来	down [used here in the "write something down" sense]
huàyǔ	话语	words, discourse
suǒyǐ	所以	so
zūnzhào	遵照	in accordance with
yìzhì	意志	will [the noun, as in "God's will" or "your will be done"]
xiěxià de	写下的	written down
héxié	和谐	harmonious
tǒngyī	统一	unity, unified

Translation:

Lesson 6: The Bible

The Bible is a letter God wrote to humanity, it is God's words revealed to some people, and these people used a pen to record them. So the Bible is written down by people according to God's will and his words are harmonious and unified.

第七课：祷告

"祷告"的意思是"跟神说话。"任何人都能祷告。如果你想祷告，那是很简单的：你可以对神畅所欲言！神会听见你的每一句话。你不需要用正式或者专业的言语。

dì qī	第七	seventh
dǎogào	祷告	prayer, to pray
yìsī	意思	meaning
gēn	跟	with
shuōhuà	说话	to speak
rènhé rén	任何人	anybody [literally "any person"]
dōu	都	all
néng	能	to be able to
nà	那	that
hěn	很	very
jiǎndān	简单	simple
kěyǐ	可以	can
duì	对	to
chàngsuǒyùyán	畅所欲言	to speak one's heart freely
tīngjiàn	听见	to hear
měi yī jù huà	每一句话	every word

měi yī	每一	every [sometimes 一 is left off and you will just see 每]
jù	句	[measure word for words, phrases, and utterances]
huà	话	spoken word or words
xūyào	需要	to need
yòng	用	to use
zhèngshì	正式	formal, official
huòzhě	或者	or
zhuānyè	专业	professional
yányǔ	言语	language

Translation:

Lesson 7: Prayer

"Prayer" means "talking with God." Anybody can pray. If you want to pray, it is very simple: you can just talk to Him like a friend! God will hear your every word. You do not need to use formal or professional speech.

第八课：丰盛的生命

我们生命的目的是跟神建立关系。虽然我们有很多钱，但是如果我们没有跟神建立关系，我们的心灵会很空虚。这些物质的东西不能帮我们认识神，所以不能让我们满足。

dì bā	第八	eighth
fēngshèng	丰盛	rich, prosperous
shēngmìng	生命	life
mùdì	目的	goal, objective
jiànlì	建立	to establish
guānxì	关系	relationship
suīrán...dànshì	虽然...但是	even though...but
hěn duō	很多	very much
qián	钱	money
xīnlíng	心灵	soul
kōngxū	空虚	empty, hollow
wùzhì	物质	physical, material
dōngxī	东西	stuff, things [physical objects]
bāng	帮	to help
rènshì	认识	to meet, to know
ràng	让	to make

mǎnzú　　　满足　　　satisfied

Translation:

Lesson 8: Prosperous Life

The goal of our lives is to have a relationship with God. Even though [used here, the best translation is probably closer to "Even if"] we have a lot of money, but if we do not have a relationship with God, our souls will be empty. These material things cannot help us know God, so they cannot make us satisfied.

第九课：神超越文化

基督教是超越文化的，因为神是超越文化的。他是全世界的主，全世界的创造者。全世界都应当敬拜神。

dì jiǔ	第九	ninth
chāoyuè	超越	to transcend
wénhuà	文化	culture
jīdūjiào	基督教	Christianity
quán shìjiè	全世界	the whole world
quán	全	complete
zhǔ	主	Lord
chuàngzàozhě	创造者	creator
chuàngzào	创造	to create
zhě	[verb]者	one who does [verb], [verb]er — so here it means "one who creates," or "creator"
yīngdāng	应当	ought to, must, should
jìngbài	敬拜	to worship

Translation:

Lesson 9: God Transcends Culture

Christianity transcends culture, because God transcends

culture. He is the Lord of the whole world, the creator of the whole world. The whole world should worship Him.

第十课：中国基督徒

我知道大部分的中国人不是基督徒，但是我已经认识了很多中国基督徒！从过去四百年到现在，一直连续不断的有中国人决定成为基督徒。

pinyin	汉字	English
dì shí	第十	tenth
zhōngguó	中国	China
jīdūtú	基督徒	Christian [as in a Christian person or persons]
zhīdào	知道	to know
dàbùfēn	大部分	the majority of
zhōngguórén	中国人	Chinese people
yǐjīng	已经	already
rènshì	认识	to meet, to know
cóng guòqù...dào xiànzài	从过去...到现在	from the past...till now [or "for the past X amount of time"]
sì bǎi	四百	four hundred
nián	年	year
dào	到	to
xiànzài	现在	now
yīzhí	一直	continuously, always
liánxùbùduàn	连续不断	continuously
juédìng	决定	to decide

chéngwéi　　　成为　　　to become

Translation:

Lesson 10: Chinese Christians

I know the majority of Chinese people are not Christians, but I have already met many Chinese Christians! In the past four hundred years, there have continuously been Chinese people deciding to become Christians.

第十一课：无神论是一种信仰

没有宗教信仰的人往往以为他们不信超自然的东西，所以他们没有信仰。但是"信仰"不但描写一个人信什么宗教，而且描写一个人有什么世界观，用什么方法决定怎么样生活。每个人都有一种世界观，都有一个方法决定怎么样生活，所以每个人都有一种信仰。

dì shí yī	第十一	eleventh
wúshénlùn	无神论	atheism
yīzhǒng	一种	a kind of, a type of
zhǒng	种	kind, type
xìnyǎng	信仰	faith [usually religious faith]
zōngjiào	宗教	religion, religious
wǎngwǎng	往往	often
yǐwéi	以为	to think erroneously
bùxìn	不信	to disbelieve, to not believe in

xìn	信		to believe [compare with the meaning of 信 in Lesson 6 — it can mean both "letter" and "to believe" depending on the context]
chāo zìrán	超自然		supernatural
dōngxī	东西		stuff [physical objects]
bùdàn...érqiě	不但...而且		not only...but also
miáoxiě	描写		to describe
yīgè rén	一个人		a person
shénme	什么		what
shìjièguān	世界观		worldview
fāngfǎ	方法		method
zěnmeyàng	怎么样		how, what kind [sometimes 样 is omitted — when this happens, 怎么 just means "how"]
shēnghuó	生活		life, to live

Translation:

Lesson 11: Atheism is a Kind of Faith

People without a religious faith often erroneously think that because they do not believe in supernatural things, they do not have faith. But "faith" does not only describe a person's religion. It also describes a person's worldview, and what method they use to decide how to live. Every person has a worldview and a way of deciding how to live, so every person has a kind of faith.

第二部分
Part Two*

*These next lessons are more advanced. Do not be alarmed if you need to go through them more slowly. Lessons 12-16 are a detailed 5-part Gospel presentation, and as such are particularly dense. I've included them early because most people prioritize learning to share the Gospel, but if you find yourself discouraged, do not be afraid to skip these lessons and come back to them later. You will probably find lessons 17-26 to be slightly easier. Note: vocabulary words will now be underlined, and after some lessons I will include supplementary memory verses related to the passage. Don't worry about memorizing the Chinese in the Bible verses; the important thing is to memorize the scripture reference and the basic content (in English). If you know these, you can always show someone the passage in a Chinese Bible.

第十二课:"没有人能证明神是否存在,所以你为什么相信他存在?"

你说得对,没有人能证明神的存在,但是没有人能证明他不存在。所以我们该怎么办呢?

我自己觉得相信神的存在是最有逻辑的看法。如果神不存在,宇宙从哪里来?我们人类的道德是谁教的?还有大自然有很多复杂的东西。比如说,一个人的大脑比电脑复杂的多。我们一看电脑就知道它是被一个很聪明的人创造了的。因此,我们一看一个人就知道他是被伟大的神创造了的。

zhèngmíng	证明	to prove
shìfǒu	是否	whether
cúnzài	存在	to exist
wéishénme	为什么	why

xiāngxìn	相信	to believe (in)
shuō de duì	说得对	to speak correctly
shuō	说	to speak
de	得	[indicates the next word is an adverb or adjective]
duì	对	correct
gāi	该	should, short for 应该
zěnmebàn	怎么办	what to do?
ne	呢	[indicates sentence is a question]
zìjǐ	自己	myself, by myself
juéde	觉得	to think
zuì yǒu luójí	最有逻辑	having the most logic
zuì	最	[makes the following word/phrase a superlative]
luójí	逻辑	logic
kànfǎ	看法	perspective
cóng nǎlǐ lái	从哪里来	where did [subject] come from?
cóng	从	from
nǎlǐ	哪里	where?
lái	来	to come
dàodé	道德	morals
shéi	谁	who?
jiào	教	to teach
háiyǒu	还有	also [literally "still to have"]
dàzìrán	大自然	nature, natural
fùzá	复杂	complicated
bǐrú shuō	比如说	for example

dànǎo	大脑	brain
bǐ...de duō	比[noun+adj]的多	much more [adj] than [noun] — [so here the phrase means "much more complicated than a computer"]
diànnǎo	电脑	computer
yī kàn...jiù	一看[noun]就	as soon as one looks at [noun]
kàn	看	to look, to see
zhīdào	知道	to know
tā	它	it
bèi	被	by [used to indicate passive voice]
cōngmíng	聪明	wise, clever
yīncǐ	因此	therefore
wěidà	伟大	great, mighty

Translation:

Lesson 12: "Nobody can prove whether God exists, so why do you believe He exists?"

What you said is right: nobody can prove God exists. But nobody can prove He doesn't exist. So what should we do?

I think that believing God exists is the most logical perspective. If God does not exist, where did the universe come from? Who taught humanity our morals? Also, nature has many complicated things. For example, a person's brain is far more complicated than a computer. When we see a computer, we know it was made by a very clever person. Therefore, when we see a person we can know that he was made by a great God.

Supplemental Memory Verse

罗马书 1:19-20 (Chinese Standard Bible (Simplified) (CSBS))
19 实际上，有关神的事，人所能知道的，在他们里面是清清楚楚的，因为神已经向他们显明了。 20 原来，自从创世以来，神那不可见的本性，就是他永恒的大能和神性，都藉着所造之物，被人明白、被人看见，以致使人无法推诿。

Romans 1:19-20 (English Standard Version (ESV))
19 For what can be known about God is plain to them, because God has shown it to them. 20 For his invisible attributes, namely, his eternal power and divine nature, have been clearly perceived, ever since the creation of the world, in the things that have been made. So they are without excuse.

第十三课:"神是什么?神有什么样的品质?"

神是无所不在、无所不知、无所不能的。神创造了宇宙万物;神绝对完美,配得尊崇;神了解你我,甚至知道我们内心所有的想法,最大的希望,最黑暗的秘密,和最深的绝望。纵然神那么圣洁和伟大,他依然深爱着你和我。神想跟每个人建立关系。

yàng	样	kind, type
pǐnzhì	品质	quality, character
wú suǒ bù zài	无所不在	omnipresent [literally "nowhere [God] is not"]
wú suǒ bù zhī	无所不知	all-knowing [literally "nothing [God] does not know"]
wú suǒ bù néng	无所不能	omnipotent, almighty [literally "nothing [God] cannot do"]
yǔ zhòu wàn wù	宇宙万物	universe [basically means the same as 宇宙]
juéduì	绝对	absolute, absolutely

wánměi	完美	perfect
pèide	配得	worthy
zūnchóng	尊崇	respected, honored
liǎojiě	了解	to understand [implies deep, comprehensive understanding]
shènzhì	甚至	even
nèi xīn	内心	inner heart
suǒyǒu	所有	all, every
xiǎngfǎ	想法	thought, idea, view
dà	大	big
xīwàng	希望	hope, to hope
hēi'àn	黑暗	dark
mìmì	秘密	secret
shēn	深	deep
juéwàng	绝望	despair
zòngrán	纵然	despite
nàme	那么	that, so
shèngjí	圣洁	holy
yīrán	依然	still, as before
shēn'ài	深爱	to love deeply
ài	爱	to love
zhe	着	[used to indicate the preceding verb/action is ongoing]

Translation:

Lesson 13: "What is God? What kind of character does He have?"

God is omnipresent, all-knowing, and able to do anything.

[Literally, these phrases mean something closer to "There is nowhere God is not, nothing He does not know, and nothing he cannot do."] God created the universe; He is absolutely perfect, and worthy of reverence. God understands you and me. He even understands all our inner heart's thoughts, biggest hopes, darkest secrets, and deepest despairs. Even though God is so holy and great, He still deeply loves you and me. God wants to have a relationship with every person.

Supplemental Memory Verse

诗篇 139:1-6 (Chinese Union Version Modern Punctuation (Simplified) (CUVMPS))
1 耶和华啊,你已经鉴察我,认识我。
2 我坐下,我起来,你都晓得,你从远处知道我的意念。

Psalm 139:1-6 (ESV)
1 O Lord, you have searched me and known me!
2 You know when I sit down and when I rise up;
 you discern my thoughts from afar.

第十四课：人类的问题

但是有一个问题。神是完美的，而人类是有罪的。我说的"罪"包括我们做的不好的事情，还有我们心里邪恶的态度。比如说，我从来没有杀死过一个人，但是我恨过人。对神来说，杀人是罪，恨人也是罪；偷东西是罪，妒忌也是罪。

因此，你看：世界上所有的人肯定都有罪，难道不是吗？只有神是完美的！一个罪也没有。神当然不能跟我们有罪的人有关系。那我们该怎么办？我们怎么能认识神呢？

wèntí	问题	problem
ér	而	but
zuì	罪	sin
bāokuò	包括	to include
zuò	做	to do

shìqíng	事情	stuff [abstract, non-material]
xīnlǐ	心里	in one's heart
xié'è	邪恶	evil
tàidù	态度	attitude
cóng lái méi yǒu	从来没有	to have never done [something]
shāsǐguò	杀死过	to have murdered
shāsǐ	杀死	to murder
guò	过	[used after a verb to indicate the subject has done the verb before]
hènguò	恨过	to have hated
hèn	恨	hate, to hate
duì...lái shuō	对...来说	according to
shārén	杀人	murder, to murder a person
hènrén	恨人	hate, to hate a person
yě	也	also
tōu	偷	to steal
dùjì	妒忌	to envy, to be jealous
kěndìng	肯定	certainly, definitely
nán dào bù shì mā?	难道不是吗?	a rhetorical "isn't it so?" [expects the answer "yes"]
mā	吗	indicates sentence is a question
zhǐ	只	just, only
yī gè...yě méi yǒu	一个[noun]也没有	to have not even one [noun]
dāngrán	当然	of course

nà	那	[sometimes used at the beginning of a question to make it more informal]
gāi	该	should
rènshi	认识	to meet, to know
ne	呢	[indicates sentence is a question]

Translation:

Lesson 14: Humanity's Problem

But there is a problem. God is perfect, but humanity is sinful. The "sin" I am talking about includes bad things we do, and also the evil attitudes in our hearts. For example, I have never killed a person, but I sometimes hate people. According to God, killing a person is sin, but hating a person is also sin. Stealing stuff is sin, but envying is also sin.

Therefore, you can see that everybody in the world certainly is sinful, isn't that so? But God is perfect, without a single fault! Of course He cannot have a relationship with sinful humanity. What are we to do? How can we meet God?

Supplemental Memory Verse

罗马书 3:23 (CSBS)
23 要知道，每个人都犯了罪，亏缺了神的荣耀

Romans 3:23 (ESV)
23 for all have sinned and fall short of the glory of God

第十五课:"谁能解决这个问题?"

神已经为解决这个问题预备了方法。两千多年前,神的爱子耶稣基督,进入我们的宇宙,成为一个有肉身的人类。耶稣基督住在地球上三十多年,用他完美的无罪的人性,用他绝对的超然的神性,用人类的样式和方法启示怎样和神建立关系。耶稣基督用他一人的死,成为人类罪的赎价。

神为什么让耶稣牺牲了?因为神是完美的,圣洁的和公义的,所以他要求我们为我们的罪付出代价。我们罪的代价就是死亡和跟神永远的分离。但是他没有把我们处罚,反而他让耶稣牺牲了。耶稣替我们付了罪的代价。罪的代价是死亡,所以耶稣为我们牺牲他的生命,赎了我们的

zuì gěi le wǒ men xīn de shēng mìng
罪，给了我们新的生命。

yé sū sǐ le sān tiān yǐ hòu cóng sǐ lǐ fù huó le rán hòu lí kāi shì jiè huí tiān táng qù le
耶稣死了三天以后，从死里复活了！然后离开世界回天堂去了。

shéi	谁	who?
jiějué	解决	to solve
wéi	为	for
yùbèi	预备	to prepare
fāngfǎ	方法	method
liǎng qiān duō nián	两千多年	over 2000 years
liǎng qiān	两千	2000
duō	多	more than, over [goes after the number]
nián	年	year
qián	前	before, ago
àizǐ	爱子	beloved child
jìnrù	进入	to enter
chéngwéi	成为	to become
ròushēn	肉身	flesh, incarnate, "flesh-and-blood"
zhù	住	to live
dìqiú	地球	the earth, planet Earth
yòng	用	to use, to apply
wú zuì	无罪	sinless

wú	无	without
rénxìng	人性	humanity
juéduì	绝对	absolute
chāorán	超然	supernatural
shénxìng	神性	divinity
yàngshì	样式	style
zěnyàng	怎样	how
shújià	赎价	ransom
ràng	让	to allow, to compel
xīshēng	牺牲	to sacrifice
shèngjí	圣洁	holy
gōngyì	公义	justice
yàoqiú	要求	to require, requirement
fùchū	付出	to pay out
dàijià	代价	price
sǐwáng	死亡	death
fēnlí	分离	separation
bǎ	把	[used after the subject but before the object to create an SOV sentence: Subject->把->Object->Verb]
chǔfá	处罚	to punish
fǎn'ér	反而	on the contrary
tì	替	on behalf of, for
fù	付	to pay
shú	赎	to redeem, to atone redemption
sǐ	死	to die
yǐhòu	以后	after, later

cóng sǐlǐ fùhuó le	从死里复活了	"resurrected from the dead" [you should memorize this phrase; there's really no good way to talk around it if you don't know it]
cóng	从	from
sǐ lǐ	死里	death [literally "in death"]
fùhuó	复活	to resurrect
líkāi	离开	to leave
huí [place] qù	回[place]去	to return to [place]
tiāntáng	天堂	Heaven

Translation:

Lesson 15: "Who can solve this problem?"

God has already prepared a way to solve this problem. 2000 years ago, God's beloved son, Jesus Christ, entered our universe and become a flesh-and-blood human. Jesus lived on the earth for over 30 years, and used his perfect sinless human nature, used his absolutely transcendently divine nature, and used humanity's styles and methods to reveal how to have a relationship with God. [This sentence is really awkward in English, but I promise it sounds better in Chinese]. Jesus Christ used his own death to become the ransom for humanity's sin.

Why did God allow Jesus to be sacrificed? Because God is perfect, just, and righteous, He requires us to pay the price for our sin. The punishment for our sin is death, and eternal separation from God. But He did not punish us, instead He allowed Jesus to be executed. Jesus paid the price for our sins. The price of sin is death, so Jesus sacrificed his life for us, atoned for our sins, and gave us new life.

Three days after Jesus died, he resurrected from the dead! Afterward, he left the world and returned to heaven.

Supplemental Memory Verse

罗马书 5:8-9 (CSBS)
8但是，当我们还是罪人的时候，基督就替我们死了。神的爱就在此向我们显明了。9所以，我们现在既然藉着基督的血被称为义，难道不更要藉着他，从神的震怒中被拯救出来吗？

Romans 5:8-9 (ESV)
8 but God shows his love for us in that while we were still sinners, Christ died for us. 9 Since, therefore, we have now been justified by his blood, much more shall we be saved by him from the wrath of God.

第十六课：你的决定

但是只知道这些事情是不够的。如果你想经历新的生命，你就需要相信耶稣基督真的赎清了你的罪，告诉神你愿意接受这个新生命，和承诺在这个新生命里你不想"走自己的路，"反而想跟随神，想服从他的命令。

如果你同意，你可以做这个祷告（"祷告"的意思只是对神说）：

"神，我是一个有罪的人。我不能赎自己的罪，不能和你有关系。但是我很感谢你让你儿子来到世界，替我付了罪的代价。我接受你送给我的新生命。从现在起，我不想走自己的路，但是想跟随你，服从你的命令。我很感谢你，我敬拜你，奉主耶稣基督的名祷告，阿门。"

juédìng	决定	decision, to decide
bùgòu	不够	not enough
gòu	够	enough
shúqīng	赎清	to redeem [same as 赎]
gàosù	告诉	to tell
yuànyì	愿意	to be willing
jiēshòu	接受	to accept, to receive, to take
chéngnuò	承诺	commitment, to commit
lǐ	里	in, inside
fúcóng	服从	to obey
mìnglìng	命令	instructions
tóngyì	同意	to agree
gǎnxiè	感谢	to thank, thanks
sòng gěi wǒ de	送给我的	"freely given to me"
sòng gěi	送给	to give freely
cóng xiànzài qǐ	从现在起	from now on
jìngbài	敬拜	to worship
fèng	奉	in the name of [used in reference to kings, emperors, etc.]
míng	名	name [short for 名字]
āmén	阿门	Amen

Translation:

Lesson 16: Your Decision

But just knowing these things is not enough. If you want to experience new life, you must believe that Jesus actually atoned for your sins, tell God that you are willing to accept this new life, and commit that in this new life you do not want to "walk your own road," but instead want to follow God and obey his commands.

If you agree, you can pray this prayer ("prayer" just means talking to God):

"God, I am a sinful person. By myself, I cannot atone for my own sins or have a relationship with you. But I am very grateful to you for sending your son to the world to pay the price for my sin. I receive the new life you give me. From now on, I do not want to go my own way, but want to follow you and obey your commands. I am very grateful to you; I worship you. In the name of Lord Jesus Christ I pray, Amen."

Supplemental Memory Verses

约翰福音 3:16 (CSBS)
16 神爱世人，甚至赐下他的独生子，好让所有信他的人不至于灭亡，反得永恒的生命

John 3:16 (ESV)
16 For God so loved the world, that he gave his only Son, that whoever believes in him should not perish but have eternal life.

哥林多后书 5:17 (CSBS)
17 因此，如果有人在基督里，他就是新造的人；旧的已经过去，看哪，新的已经来临。

2 Corinthians 5:17
17 Therefore, if anyone is in Christ, he is a new creation. The old has passed away; behold, the new has come.

第十七课:"我生命的目的是赚很多钱,买房子,买车子,结婚,生小孩。如果我得到这些,我肯定会感到非常满足。"

你刚才说的话很有意思,但是我有不同的看法。我来自美国,美国是一个发达国家,大部分的美国人有车子,有房子,等等……

如果按照你的道理,大部分的美国人一定非常满足,不是吗?但是不是这样的。在美国,自杀是一个很大的社会问题。绝望是很普遍的,特别是有钱的人。有不少非常成功的明星自杀了。

为什么会这样?我自己觉得是因为我们生命真正的目标并不是为了取得成功,不是赚钱，不是找到丈夫或者妻子，不是买东西，也不是生小孩。我们生命的目标是跟神建立关系。即使我们取得"成功，"但是如果我们没有跟神有关系，我们的心灵会很空虚。这些物质的东西是不能帮我们认识神的，所以不能让我们满足。

zhuàn	赚	to earn
qián	钱	money
mǎi	买	to buy
fángzi	房子	house, apartment
chēzi	车子	car, vehicle
jiéhūn	结婚	to marry
shēng xiǎohái	生小孩	to give birth to a child
dédào	得到	to get, to obtain
huì	会	will be
gǎndào	感到	to feel
fēicháng	非常	very, extremely
mǎnzú	满足	satisfied, to satisfy, satisfaction, contentment
gāngcái	刚才	just now
hěn yǒu yìsī	很有意思	very interesting
bùtóng	不同	different [literally "not the same"]

kànfǎ	看法	perspective
lái zì	来自	to come from
měiguó	美国	the United States
fādá	发达	developed
guójiā	国家	country
dàbùfēn	大部分	the majority
děngděng	等等	etc.
ànzhào	按照	according to
dàolǐ	道理	truth
yīdìng	一定	certainly, certain
bù shì mā?	不是吗?	right? [rhetorical question, expects the answer 是]
zìshā	自杀	suicide
shèhuì	社会	society, societal
juéwàng	绝望	despair
pǔbiàn	普遍	common
tèbié	特别	especially, special
yǒu qián de rén	有钱的人	rich people
bù shǎo	不少	many, not a few
shǎo	少	few
chénggōng	成功	success
míngxīng	明星	celebrity, star
zhēnzhèng	真正	actual, real
mùbiāo	目标	goal, objective [basically the same as 目的]
qǔdé	取得	to achieve
zhǎodào	找到	to find
zhàngfū	丈夫	husband
qīzi	妻子	wife

jíshǐ	即使	even if
xīnlíng	心灵	soul
kōngxū	空虚	empty, hollow

Translation:

Lesson 17: "The point of my life is to earn money, buy an apartment, by a car, marry, and have a child. If I achieve these things, I certainly will feel very satisfied."

What you just said is very interesting. But I have a different perspective. I come from America, and America is a developed nation, so the majority of Americans have a car, a house, etc.

If what you say is true [literally, "If according to your truth"], the majority of Americans will be very satisfied, right? But this is actually not the case. In America suicide is a big societal problem. Despair is very common, especially among wealthy people. There are not a few extremely successful celebraties who have killed themselves.

Why is this? I think this is because the actual purpose of our lives is not to achieve success, is not to earn money, is not to find a husband or a wife, is not to buy things, and is not to have children. The purpose of our lives is to have a relationship with God. Even if we achieve "success," if we do not have a relationship with God, our souls will be empty. These material things cannot help us meet God, so they cannot satisfy us.

第十八课:"所有的美国人都是基督徒,对吗?"

根据一些调查,大概百分之八十的美国人信基督教。但是如果一个人说他信基督教,他不一定是真正的基督徒。他需要相信福音和跟随神。如果他不相信福音,不跟随神,他其实并不是基督徒,即使他说他是基督徒。

基督教对美国的文化有很大的影响,所以现在很多美国人以为他们是基督徒但是他们不信福音。这样的人不是基督徒。我所谓的百分之八十的美国人口包括很多这样的人。

美国的情况可能跟中国的有点儿一样,是不是?在中国好像有很多人,特别是年

<u>轻</u>人，说他们信<u>佛教</u>，但是他们<u>却</u>不了解佛教的<u>信仰</u>。

jīdūtú	基督徒	a Christian person(s)
duì ma?	对吗？	right? [rhetorical question expecting the answer "yes"]
gēn jù	根据	according to
diàochá	调查	survey
dàgài	大概	about, approximately
bǎi fēn zhī bāshí	百分之八十	80%
bǎi fēn zhī	百分之	[used to indicate a percent, but precedes the number instead of following it like % does in English]
bāshí	八十	80
jīdūjiāo	基督教	Christianity, the Christian religion
bù yīdìng	不一定	not necessarily
fúyīn	福音	the Gospel, literally "blessed sound"
qíshí	其实	actually
jíshǐ	即使	even if
wénhuà	文化	culture
yǐngxiǎng	影响	influence
hěn duō	很多	very many
zhèyàng	这样	this kind of, this type of
rénkǒu	人口	population
qíngkuàng	情况	situation

kěnéng	可能	maybe
diǎn'ér*	点儿	a little bit
yīyàng	一样	the same, similar
hǎoxiàng	好像	it seems that
niánqīng	年轻	young
fójiāo	佛教	Buddhism
què	却	actually, in actuality
xìnyǎng	信仰	faith

*this is pronounced "diar" (like "dee are" but combined into one syllable)

Translation:

Lesson 18: "All Americans are Christians, right?"

According to some surveys, about 80% of Americans believe Christianity. But just because a person says he believes Christianity, he is not necessarily a Christian. He must believe in the Gospel and follow God. If a person does not believe the Gospel and follow God, then even if he says he is a Christian, he actually isn't a Christian.

Christianity has had a great influence on American culture, so right now there are many Americas who erroneously think they are Christians, but they don't believe the Gospel. This kind of person is not a Christian. The 80% of Americans I spoke of earlier includes many of these kind of people.

America's situation is a little similar to China's situation, isn't it? In China, it seems like there are a lot of people, especially young people, who say they believe in Buddhism, but are not familiar with the Buddhist faith.

Note:

This lesson about whether or not all Americans are Christian may seem like a weird passage to include, but it's actually pretty important. I can't count the number of times a Chinese person asked me this question while I was in Asia. Often the best response is simply to say "not necessarily," but if the situation is appropriate to give a longer answer, the passage in this lesson can be helpful because it communicates three valuable truths. First, it implies that a person's religious beliefs are independent of her culture; just because someone is from a country with a Christian heritage does not mean she is a Christian. Second, it states that merely claiming to be a Christian doesn't automatically make someone a Christian. Third, it provides a simple definition of "Christian" — someone who believes in the Gospel and follows God. (This gives you the chance to share the Gospel if your friend asks what it is). These three truths can be a great foundation for future discussions, and can efficiently clear up several common misconceptions.

第十九课："我没有信仰，我只相信我自己。"

那太好了！我也相信我自己！但是这个不是信仰，只是自信。自信肯定很重要，有很大的力量，但是在我们生命当中自信和信仰有不同的角色。

我不能依靠自己让我的生命有意义，或者有一个满足的生活。有时候我有一些生活习惯我想改变，但是我凭自己改不了。满足这些需要是信仰的角色。

nà tài hǎo le	那太好了	"that is so good"
nà	那	that
tài...le	太[adj]了	extremely [adjective], too [adjective]
zìxìn	自信	self-confidence
kěndìng	肯定	certainly
zhòngyào	重要	important
lìliang	力量	power

dāngzhōng	当中		in [used to mean being "in" something abstract, such as "life"]
juésè	角色		role
yīkào	依靠		to rely on
yìyì	意义		meaning, significance
shēnghuó	生活		life, livelihood
yǒu shíhòu	有时候		sometimes [literally "there are times"]
shíhòu	时候		time
xíguàn	习惯		habit
gǎibiàn	改变		to change
píng	凭		to rely on
gǎi	改		to change [short for 改变]
bù liǎo	[verb]不了		to be unable to do [verb]
xūyào	需要		need [here it is a noun]

Translation:

Lesson 19: "I do not have a religious faith, I just believe in myself."

Oh that's very good! I also believe in myself! But this is not faith, just self-confidence. Self-confidence is definitely very important and has great power. But in our lives, self-confidence and faith have different roles.

By myself I cannot make my life have meaning, or have a satisfying life. Sometimes I have life habits I want to change, but I cannot change them by relying on myself. Satisfying these needs is the role of faith.

第二十课:"圣经是什么?"

圣经是一封神写给人类的信,是神启示给一些人然后这些人用笔记录下来的话语。所以圣经是人遵照神的意志写下的和谐统一的话语。

神为什么赐给我们圣经?那是因为神爱我们,想跟我们建立关系。圣经是一本人生说明书,目的是向我们介绍神,告诉我们怎么能跟他建立关系,教我们最好的办法来度过我们的生命。

圣经有两部分:第一部分告诉我们耶稣基督降世界以前,神做了什么。这部分叫"旧约。"第二部分告诉我们耶稣基督降世界以后,神做了什么。这部分叫"新约。"

如果你从来没看过圣经，我建议你看新约里的"马可福音，"因为它清楚地描写了耶稣基督的生命。

jìlù	记录	to record
zūnzhào	遵照	in accordance with
yìzhì	意志	will [the noun, as in "God's will" or "your will be done"]
héxié	和谐	harmony, harmonious
tǒngyī	统一	unity, unified
huàyǔ	话语	speech, words, discorse
cìgěi	赐给	to give, to bestow upon [literally "to give by means of bestowing"]
cì	赐	to bestow
yī běn rénshēng shuōmíng shū	一本人生说明书	"a life instruction-manual"
běn	本	[measure word for books]
rénshēng	人生	life
shuōmíng	说明	directions, explanation, to explain
shū	书	book
xiàng	向	to
jièshào	介绍	to introduce

dùguò	度过	to spend
bùfēn	部分	part
jiàng	降	to drop, to come down
yǐqián	以前	before, ago
jiào	叫	to be called, to be named
jiùyuē	旧约	the Old Testament
yǐhòu	以后	after
xīnyuē	新约	the New Testament
cóng lái méi kàn guò	从来没看过	have never read [when using 看 with a book it means "to read"]
jiànyì	建议	to suggest
Mǎkě fúyīn	马可福音	the Gospel of Mark
Mǎkě	马可	Mark
fúyīn	福音	Gospel
qīngchǔ	清楚	clearly
miáoxiě	描写	to describe

Translation:

Lesson 20: "What is the Bible?"

The Bible is a letter God wrote to humanity, it is God's words revealed to some people, and these people used a pen to record them. So the Bible is written down by people according to God's will and his words are harmonious and unified.

Why did God give us the Bible? It is because he loves us and he wants a relationship with us. The Bible is a life instruction manual, the goal of which is to introduce us to God, tell us how to have a relationship with Him, and teach us the best way to spend our lives.

The Bible has two parts: the first part teaches us what God did before Jesus Christ came down to the world. This part is called the Old Testament. The second part teaches us what God did after Jesus Christ came down to the world. This part is called the New Testament.

If you have never read the Bible, I suggest you start with "Mark" in the New Testament because it clearly describes Jesus' life.

第二十一课："基督教和中国文化有矛盾吗？"

我们需要清楚地分别"文化"和"信仰"是什么。"文化"只描述一个社会中的人一般做的是什么。他们喜欢听什么样的音乐，看什么样的书，有什么传统，等等。"信仰"跟道理有关系，描述一个人有什么世界观。

基督教超越文化，因为神超越文化。他是全世界的主，全世界的创造者，所以全世界应该敬拜他。基督教跟任何社会的文化没有矛盾。

但是基督教是独特的，和其他的信仰不一样。因为信仰与客观真理有关，所以只能有一个正确的信仰。因此，基督教和其他的信仰（包括佛教，无神论，伊斯兰教，等等）有矛盾。

pinyin	汉字	English
máodùn	矛盾	conflict
qīngchǔ de	清楚地	clearly
de	地	[used to indicate the preceding word is an adverb]
fēnbié	分别	to differentiate or distinguish
miáoshù	描述	to describe [similar in meaning to 描写]
zhōng	[noun]中	in [noun]
yībān	一般	usually
xǐhuān	喜欢	to like, to enjoy
tīng	听	to listen
yīnyuè	音乐	music
chuántǒng	传统	tradition
shìjièguān	世界观	worldview
chāoyuè	超越	to transcend
dútè	独特	unique, one-of-a-kind
qítā de	其他的	other
yǔ...yǒu guān	与[noun]有关	having to do with [noun]
kèguān	客观	objective, opposite of subjective
zhēnlǐ	真理	truth
zhèngquè	正确	true, correct
fójiāo	佛教	Buddhism

wúshénlùn	无神论	Atheism
yīsīlánjiāo	伊斯兰教	Islam

Translation:

Lesson 21: "Does Christianity conflict with Chinese culture?"

We must clearly distinguish "culture" from "faith." "Culture" just describes what people in a society normally do: what kind of music they like, what kind of books they read, what traditions they have, etc. "Faith" has to do with truth; it describes what worldview a person has.

Christianity transcends culture because God transcends culture. He is the Lord of the whole world; He created the whole world. So the whole world should worship Him. Christianity does not conflict with any society's culture.

However, Christianity is one-of-a-kind; it is not like other faiths. Because faith concerns objective truth, there can only be one correct faith. Therefore, Christianity has a conflict with other religions (including Buddhism, Atheism, Islam, etc.)

Supplemental Memory Verse

启示录 7:9-10 (CSBS)
9 这些事以后，我观看，看哪，有一大群人，没有人能够数过来。他们来自各国家、各支派、各民族、各语言群体。他们身穿白袍，手里拿着棕榈枝，站在宝座和羔羊面前， 10 大声呼喊说："救恩属于坐在宝座上我们的神、属于羔羊！"

Revelation 7:9-10 (ESV)
9 After this I looked, and behold, a great multitude that no one could number, from every nation, from all tribes and peoples and languages, standing before the throne and before the Lamb, clothed in white robes, with palm branches in their hands, 10 and crying out with a loud voice, "Salvation belongs to our God who sits on the throne, and to the Lamb!"

第二十二课："基督教和科学是矛盾的吗？"

我信基督教，但是我也信科学。我看不到矛盾。

基督教和科学都跟客观的真理有关系，但是有不同的目的：它们回答的是不同的问题。科学集中回答"怎么？"但是基督教集中回答"为什么？"

比如说宇宙源头的问题。科学是学习宇宙的起源的，现在大部分的科学家同意宇宙的开始是那个大爆炸。但是科学不能解释宇宙为什么开始。对圣经来说，宇宙开始了因为神让它开始，但是没有说他用得什么具体的办法。★

平时基督教和科学好像有矛盾的时候，其实不是矛盾，是因为它们在学习一件事情的不同方面。

★很有意思的事情：圣经和进化论有很多一样的地方。比如说基督教和科学都同意生命的出现是按照从简单的到复杂的顺序。我建议你看一看圣经里面的"创世纪。"那里有基督教关于世界源头的解释。

kēxué	科学	science
kàn bù dào	看不到	cannot see, to be unable to see [if you want to say "to be able to see," it's 看得到]
kèguān	客观	objective, opposite of subjective
zhēnlǐ	真理	truth
huídá	回答	to answer
jízhōng	集中	to concentrate (on)
yuántóu	源头	source, origin
xuéxí	学习	to study
qǐyuán	起源	origin

kāishǐ	开始	start, to start
dàbàozhà	大爆炸	the Big Bang
jiěshì	解释	explanation, to explain
jùtǐ	具体	specific
bànfǎ	办法	method, way of doing something
píngshí	平时	usually
hǎoxiàng	好像	to seem like, to appear
zài	在	[here used to indicate an action is continuing]
jiàn	件	[measure word commonly used with 事情]
fāngmiàn	方面	aspect, side
jìnhuàlùn	进化论	the theory of evolution
dìfāng	地方	place, thing
chūxiàn	出现	emergence, appearance
ànzhào	按照	according to
jiǎndān	简单	simple
fùzá	复杂	complex, complicated
shùnxù	顺序	ordered, in succession
kàn yī kàn	看一看	to take a look [less formal than 看, and implies a that the look will be quick]
Chuàngshìjì	创世纪	the Book of Genesis
guānyú	关于	having to do with

Translation:

Lesson 22: "Does Christianity conflict with science?"

I believe in Christianity, but I also believe in science. I do not see a contradiction.

Christianity and science both have to do with objective truth, but they have different goals: they answer different questions. Science concentrates on answering "how?," but Christianity concentrates on answering "why?"

Take, for example, the problem of the origin of the universe. Science studies the origin of the universe, and right now the majority of scientists agree the start of the universe was the Big Bang. But science is not able to explain why the universe began. According to the Bible, the universe started because God made it start. But it doesn't say what specific method God used.*

Usually when Christianity and science appear to contradict each other, it is actually not a contradiction, but is because the two are studying different aspects of the same thing.

*Something interesting: The Bible and evolution have many similarities. For example, the Bible and science both agree that life developed from simple to complex. I suggest you take a look at "Genesis" in the Bible. There is the Bible's description of the origin of the world.

第二十三课:"整个宇宙从哪里来?"

有三个可能的情况:1)宇宙没有源头因为它已经存在了。2)宇宙自然地开始,没有一个创造者。3)宇宙有一个创造者。

第一个情况跟科学有矛盾。大部分的科学家都同意宇宙是有源头的。

第二个情况很奇怪。如果宇宙没有创造者,宇宙怎么开始?如果来自随机巧合,为什么物理运动,动物身体结构,地球的运转,等等都很有条理?

第三个情况不但跟科学没有矛盾,而且能讲解宇宙的源头是什么:宇宙有一个创造者。

<ruby>我<rt>wǒ</rt></ruby><ruby>说<rt>shuō</rt></ruby><ruby>的<rt>de</rt></ruby><ruby>话<rt>huà</rt></ruby><ruby>不<rt>bù</rt></ruby><ruby>是<rt>shì</rt></ruby><ruby>一<rt>yī</rt></ruby><ruby>个<rt>gè</rt></ruby><ruby>证明<rt>zhèng míng</rt></ruby>，<ruby>只<rt>zhǐ</rt></ruby><ruby>是<rt>shì</rt></ruby><ruby>我<rt>wǒ</rt></ruby><ruby>自<rt>zì</rt></ruby><ruby>己<rt>jǐ</rt></ruby><ruby>的<rt>de</rt></ruby><ruby>看<rt>kàn</rt></ruby><ruby>法<rt>fǎ</rt></ruby>。

zhěng gè	整个	the whole, the entire
qíngkuàng	情况	situation
yuántóu	源头	origin, source
kēxuéjiā	科学家	scientist [家 when used as a suffix can mean "expert"]
qíguài	奇怪	strange
suíjī	随机	random
qiǎohé	巧合	coincidence
wùlǐ	物理	physical, physics
yùndòng	运动	motion, movement
dòngwù	动物	animal
shēntǐ jiégōu	身体结构	anatomy
shēntǐ	身体	body
jiégōu	结构	structure
dìqiú	地球	the earth, planet earth
yùnzhuǎn	运转	operations, functioning
tiáolǐ	条理	orderliness
jiǎngjiě	讲解	to explain
zhèngmíng	证明	proof, to prove

Translation:

Lesson 23: "Where did the whole universe come from?"

There are three possible situations: 1) The universe does not have an origin because it has [always] already existed. 2) The universe started naturally and does not have a creator. 3) The universe has a creator.

The first situation contradicts science. The majority of scientists agree the universe has an origin.

The second situation is very strange. If the universe does not have a creator, how did it start? If it came from random chance, why are physical motions, the anatomy of animals, the operations of the earth, etc. all so orderly?

The third situation not only does not contradict science, but also is able to explain the origin of the universe: the universe has a creator.

What I'm saying is not a proof. It's just my personal opinion.

Supplemental Memory Verse

诗篇 19:1 (CUVMPS)
1 诸天述说神的荣耀，穹苍传扬他的手段。

Psalm 19:1 (ESV)
1 The heavens declare the glory of God,
   and the sky above proclaims his handiwork.

第二十四课："基督教是不是一个西方的宗教？"

西方的文化肯定被基督教影响了，但是基督教不是从西方来的，反而它来自亚洲。神本来被犹太人敬拜，后来耶稣基督（神的儿子）在中东出生了。基督教从耶稣基督开始。

而且根据一些调查，大部分的基督徒不是西方人。世界上有大概20多亿基督徒，但是欧洲和北美一起只有8亿基督徒。其他的住在非洲，亚洲，拉美，中东，等等。在非洲百分之60的人口信基督教，在拉美百分之90人口信基督教。

xīfāng	西方	the West
zōngjiào	宗教	religion
yǐngxiǎng	影响	influence, to influence
yàzhōu	亚洲	Asia

běnlái	本来	orginally
yóutàirén	犹太人	Jewish people
hòulái	后来	later on
zhōngdōng	中东	the Middle East
chūshēng	出生	to be born
érqiě	而且	furthermore
xīfāngrén	西方人	Westerners
yì	亿	one hundred million [so that means 20亿 is 2 billion]
ōu'zhōu	欧洲	Europe
běiměi	北美	North America
yīqǐ	一起	together
fēizhōu	非洲	Africa
lāměi	拉美	Latin America

Translation:

Lesson 24: "Is Christianity a Western religion?"

Western culture definitely has been influenced by Christianity, but Christianity did not come from the West. Instead it came from Asia. God originally was worshipped by the Jewish people, and later Jesus Christ (God's son) was born in the Middle East. Christianity started from Jesus.

Furthermore, according to some surveys, the majority of Christians are not Westerners. There are about 2 billion Christians in the world, but Europe and North America combined only have about 800 million Christians. The others live in Africa, Asia, Latin America, the Middle East, etc. in Africa 60% of the population believes Christianity; in Latin America, it is 90%.

第二十五课："基督教和其他的信仰有什么不一样的地方？"

除了基督教以外，所有的宗教都说你自己应该赢得祝福的生命。对这些宗教来说，如果你做好的事情，你会有祝福的生活。但是如果你做坏的事情，你会有可悲的生活。

但是基督教完全不一样。对基督教来说，我们都做坏的事情。我们自己不能够赢得祝福的生活。很有恩典的神，从他儿子，送给我们祝福的新生活。其他的宗教都说祝福是我们赢得的，基督教说祝福是神送给我们的，我们只需要接受它。

| chú le...yǐ wài | 除了[noun]以外 | except for [noun], other than [noun], aside from [noun] |
| yíngdé | 赢得 | to earn |

zhùfú	祝福	blessed, blessing, to bless
huài	坏	bad, evil
kěbēi	可悲	miserable
bù nénggòu	不能够	to be unable to
ēndiǎn	恩典	grace, gracious

Translation:

Lesson 25: "In what ways is Christianity different from other religions?"

Except for Christianity, all religions say that you must earn the blessed life yourself. According to these religions, if you do good things, you will have a blessed life. But if you do bad things, you will have a miserable life.

But Christianity is completely different. According to Christianity, we all do bad things. By ourselves, we cannot earn a blessed life. Gracious God, through His son, gives us a blessed new life. Other religions say a blessed life is earned by us. Christianity says a blessed life is given to us by God, and we jut have to receive it.

第二十六课："如果我跟神有关系，我会有什么好处？"

跟神有关系有很多好处。基本上可以说有三种好处。

第一种是关于我们的罪。如果一个人跟神有关系，他不需要有罪恶感，因为他已经被耶稣的牺牲救赎了。即使他跟随神之前做了很多坏的行为，神不看他的罪。在他生命当中，他的罪可能还有暂时的后果，但是没有永远的后果。

第二种是关于我们的生命。如果一个人跟神有关系，他有"新生命。"他以前肯定有不少不能控制的坏习惯，比如说说谎，看色情的图像，骂人，欺骗，等等。但是神的力量比这些罪大的多！在神送给我们的新生命里，我们不是罪的奴隶。神会帮助我们逐渐改变自己的素质和行为。

第三种是关于神的爱。神真的爱我们。他的爱比亲情和友情的爱大得多。即使你生命当中没有一个朋友或者亲人，如果你跟神有关系，你不是孤独的因为神和你在一起。他了解你和爱你。

hǎochù	好处	benefit
jīběnshàng	基本上	basically
zuì'è gǎn	罪恶感	guilt, guilty feeling
xīshēng	牺牲	sacrifice, to sacrifice
jiùshú	救赎	salvation, to save
jíshǐ	即使	even if
zhīqián	之前	before
huài	坏	bad, evil, broken
xíngwéi	行为	action
zànshí	暂时	temporary
hòuguǒ	后果	consequence
yǒngyuǎn	永远	eternal
kòngzhì	控制	to control
xíguàn	习惯	habit
shuōhuǎng	说谎	to lie, to tell a lie

sèqíng	色情	pornography, pornographic
túxiàng	图像	image
màrén	骂人	to verbally assault a person
qīpiàn	欺骗	to cheat, to deceive
núlì	奴隶	slave
bāngzhù	帮助	to help
zhújiàn	逐渐	gradually
sùzhì	素质	quality (refers to the inner quality and character of a person)
xíngwéi	行为	actions, behaviors
qīnqíng	亲情	family
yǒuqíng	友情	friendship, friend
qīnrén	亲人	family member, relative
gūdú	孤独	alone
zài yīqǐ	在一起	to be together

Translation:

Lesson 26: "If I have a relationship with God, how will it benefit me?"

Having a relationship with God has many benefits. Basically, you can say there are three types of benefits.

The first has to do with our sin. If a person has a relationship with God, he does not need to have a guilty feeling for his sin because he has been saved by Jesus' sacrifice. Even if he did many bad things before he followed God, God does not look at his sin. In his life, he might have temporary consequences for his sin, but he will not have eternal consequences.

The second has to do with our lives. If a person has a relationship with God, he has "new life." Previously, he certainly had uncontrollable evil habits, such as lying, looking at pornography, cursing people, cheating, etc. But God's power is far greater than these sins! In the new life that God gives us, a person is not a slave to sin. God will help us to gradually change our character and actions.

The third has to do with God's love. God really loves us. His love is far greater than the love of other friends or relatives. Even if you do not have a single friend or relative, if you have a relationship with God, you are not alone because God is with you. He understands you and loves you.

Glossary:

ài 爱 to love
àizǐ 爱子 beloved child
āmén 阿门 Amen
ànzhào 按照 according to
bǎ 把 [used after the subject but before the object to create an SOV sentence — i.e. Subject->把->Object->Verb]
bǎi fēn zhī 百分之 [used to indicate a percent, but precedes the number instead of following it like % does in English]
bànfǎ 办法 method, way of doing something
bāng 帮 to help
bāngzhù 帮助 to help
bāokuò 包括 to include
bāshí 八十 80
bèi 被 by [used to indicate passive voice]
běiměi 北美 North America
běn 本 [measure word for books]
běnlái 本来 orginally
bǐ 笔 pen
bǐ...de duō 比[noun + adj]的多 much more [adjective] than [noun] — [so here the phrase means "much more complicated than a computer"]
bǐrú shuō 比如说 for example
bìng (1) 并 [intensifies a negation, so 并不是 is simply a more emphatic way of saying 不是]
bìng (2) 并 and, simultaneously [note in this context its meaning differs than in Lesson 3]
bù 不 [negates whatever follows it]
bù hǎo 不好 bad
bù nénggòu 不能够 to be unable to
bù shì mā? 不是吗? right? [rhetorical question, expects

the answer 是]
bù shǎo 不少 many, not a few
bù yīdìng 不一定 not necessarily
bùdàn...érqiě 不但...而且 not only...but also
bùfēn 部分 part
bùgòu 不够 insufficient, not enough
bùtóng 不同 different [literally "not the same"]
bùxìn 不信 to disbelieve, to not believe in
chàngsuǒyùyán 畅所欲言 to speak one's heart freely
chāo zìrán 超自然 supernatural
chāorán 超然 supernatural
chāoyuè 超越 to transcend
chénggōng 成功 success
chéngnuò 承诺 commitment, to commit
chéngwéi 成为 to become
chēzi 车子 car, vehicle
chú le...yǐ wài 除了[noun]以外 except for [noun], other than [noun], aside from [noun]
Chuàngshìjì 创世纪 the Book of Genesis
chuàngzào 创造 to create
chuàngzàozhě 创造者 creator
chuántǒng 传统 tradition
chǔfá 处罚 punishment, to punish
chūshēng 出生 to be born
chǔsǐ 处死 to put to death, to execute
chūxiàn 出现 emergence, appearance
cì 赐 to bestow
cìgěi 赐给 to give, to bestow upon [literally "to give by means of bestowing"]
cóng 从 from
cóng guòqù...dào xiànzài 从过去...到现在 from the past...till now [or "for the past X amount of time"]

cóng lái méi yǒu 从来没有 to have never done (something)
cóng nǎlǐ lái 从哪里来 where did [subject] come from?
cóng sǐlǐ fùhuó le 从死里复活了 "resurrected from the dead"
cóng xiànzài qǐ 从现在起 from now on
cōngmíng 聪明 wise, clever
cúnzài 存在 existence, to exist
dà 大 big
dàbàozhà 大爆炸 the Big Bang
dàbùfēn 大部分 the majority
dàgài 大概 about, approximately
dàijià 代价 price
dāngrán 当然 of course
dāngzhōng 当中 in [generally used to mean being "in" something abstract, such as "in our lives"]
dànshì 但是 but
dào 到 to
dàodé 道德 morals
dǎogào 祷告 prayer, to pray
dàolǐ 道理 truth
dàzìrán 自然 nature, natural
de 地 [used to indicate the preceding word is an adverb]
de (1) 的 [indicates the preceding word is an adjective]
de (2) 的 [possessive, equivalent to 's in English]
de 得 [indicates the next word is an adverb or adjective]
de shí hòu 的时候 at the time of, when
dédào 得到 to get, to obtain
děngděng 等等 etc.
dì bā 第八 eighth
dì jiǔ 第九 ninth
dì liù 第六 sixth

dì qī	第七	seventh
dì sān	第三	third
dì shí	第十	tenth
dì shí yī	第十一	eleventh
dì sì	第四	fourth
dì wǔ	第五	fifth
dì yī	第一	first
dì èr	第二	second
diǎn'ér	点儿	a little bit
diànnǎo	电脑	computer
diàochá	调查	survey
dìfāng	地方	place, thing
dìqiú	地球	the earth, planet Earth
dòngwù	动物	animal
dōngxī	东西	stuff [physical objects]
dòngzuò	动作	movement, action, motion
dōu	都	all
dùguò	度过	to spend
duì (1)	对	correct
duì (2)	对	to
duì…lái shuō	对…来说	according to…
duì ma?	对吗?	right? [rhetorical question expecting the answer 对]
dùjì	妒忌	to envy, to be jealous
duō	多	more than, over [goes after the number]
dútè	独特	unique, one-of-a-kind
ēndiǎn	恩典	grace, gracious
érqiě	而且	furthermore
érshì	而是	but rather
érzǐ	儿子	son
fādá	发达	developed

fǎn'ér 反而 on the contrary
fāngfǎ 方法 method
fāngmiàn 方面 aspect, side
fángzi 房子 house, apartment
fēicháng 非常 very, extremely
fēizhōu 非洲 Africa
fēnbié 分别 to differentiate or distinguish
fēng 封 [measure word for letters]
fēngshèng 丰盛 rich, prosperous
fèng 奉 in the name of [used in reference to kings, emperors, etc.]
fēnlí 分离 separation
fójiāo 佛教 Buddhism
fù 付 to pay
fùchū 付出 to pay out
fúcóng 服从 to obey
fùhuó 复活 to resurrect
fúyīn 福音 the Gospel, literally "blessed sound"
fùzá 复杂 complex, complicated
gǎi 改 to change [basically the same as 改变]
gāi 该 should
gǎibiàn 改变 to change
gǎndào 感到 to feel
gāngcái 刚才 just now
gǎnjué 感觉 feeling
gǎnxiè 感谢 to thank, thanks
gàosù 告诉 to tell
gè 个 [generic measure word]
gěi 给 to give
gēn 跟 with
gēnjù 根据 according to
gēnsuí 跟随 to follow

gōngyì 公义 justice
gòu 够 enough
guānxì 关系 relationship
guānyú 关于 having to do with
gūdú 孤独 alone
guò 过 [used after a verb to indicate the subject has done the verb before]
guójiā 国家 country
hǎi 海 ocean
háiyǒu 还有 also [literally "still to have"]
hǎo 好 good
hǎochù 好处 benefit
hǎorén 好人 good person
hǎoxiàng 好像 to seem like, to appear, it seems that
hé 和 and
hēi'àn 暗 dark
hèn 恨 hate, to hate
hěn 很 very
hěn duō 很多 many, very much
hěn yǒu yìsī 很有意思 very interesting
hènguò 恨过 to have hated
hènrén 恨人 hate, to hate
héxié 和谐 harmony, harmonious
hòuguǒ 后果 consequence
hòulái 后来 later on
huà 话 spoken word or words
huài 坏 bad, evil, broken
huàirén 坏人 bad person, evil person
huàyǔ 话语 speech, words, discorse
huì 会 will, will be
huí [place] qù 回[place]去 to return to [place]
huídá 回答 to answer

huòzhě 或者 or
jiàn 件 [measure word commonly used with 事情]
jiǎndān 简单 simple
jiàng 降 to drop, to come down
jiāng 将 [grammatical word performing a task similar to 把 — see Lesson 15]
jiǎngjiě 讲解 to explain
jiànlì 建立 to establish
jiànyì 建议 to suggest
jiào 叫 to be called, to be named
jiào 教 to teach
jīběnshàng 基本上 basically
jīdū 基督 Christ
jīdūjiào 基督教 Christianity
jīdūtú 基督徒 a Christian person(s)
jiégōu 结构 structure
jiéhūn 结婚 to marry
jiějué 解决 to solve
jièshào 介绍 to introduce
jiěshì 解释 explanation, to explain
jiēshòu 接受 to accept, to receive, to take
jìlù 记录 to record
jìnbù 进步 to progress, to develop
jìngbài 敬拜 to worship
jīnglì 经历 experience
jìnhuàlùn 进化论 the theory of evolution
jìnrù 进入 to enter
jíshǐ 即使 even if
jízhōng 集中 to concentrate
jiù 就 just
jiùshú 救赎 salvation

jiùyuē 旧约 the Old Testament
juéde 觉得 to think
juéduì 绝对 absolute, absolutely
juédìng 决定 decision, to decide
juésè 角色 role
juéwàng 绝望 despair
jù 句 [measure word for words, phrases, and utterances]
jùjué 拒绝 to refuse
jùtǐ 具体 specific
kàn 看 to look, to see
kàn bù dào 看不到 cannot see, to be unable to see [if you want to say "to be able to see," it's 看得到]
kàn yī kàn 看一看 to have a look [less formal than 看, and implies a that the look will be quick — you can do this do many verbs: verb一verb]
kànfǎ 看法 perspective
kāishǐ 开始 start, to start
kè 课 lesson
kěbēi 可悲 miserable
kèguān 客观 objective, opposite of subjective
kěndìng 肯定 certainly, definitely
kěnéng 可能 maybe
kēxué 科学 science
kēxuéjiā 科学家 scientist [家 when used as a suffix can mean "expert"]
kěyǐ 可以 can
kōngxū 空虚 empty, hollow
kòngzhì 控制 to control
lái 来 to come
lái dào 来到 to come to
lái zì 来自 to come from
lāměi 拉美 Latin America

le 了 [used after a verb to indicate the action has already happened]
lǐ 里 in, inside
liǎng qiān duō nián 两千多年 over 2000 years
liǎojiě 了解 to understand [implies deep, comprehensive understanding]
liánxùbùduàn 连续不断 continuously
líkāi 离开 to leave
lìliang 力量 power
lù 路 road
luójí 逻辑 logic
mā 吗 indicates sentence is a question
mǎi 买 to buy
Mǎkě 马可 Mark
Mǎkě fúyīn 马可福音 the Gospel of Mark
mǎnzú 满足 satisfied, to satisfy, satisfaction, contentment
máodùn 矛盾 conflict
màrén 骂人 to verbally assault a person
méi 没 [negates whatever follows it]
měi yī 每一 every [sometimes 一 is left off and you will just see 每]
měi jù huà 每句话 every word
měiguó 美国 the United States
men 们 [used to indicate more than one person]
miáoshù 描述 to describe [similar in meaning to 描写]
miáoxiě 描写 to describe
mìmì 秘密 secret
míng 名 name [short for 名字]
míngbái 明白 to understand
mìnglìng 命令 instructions
míngxīng 明星 celebrity, star

mùbiāo 目标 goal, objective [basically the same as 目的]
mùdì 目的 goal, objective
nà 那 that
nà 那 [sometimes used at the beginning of a question to make it more informal]
nà liǎng 那俩 these two
nà tài hǎo le 那太好了 "that is so good"
nǎlǐ 哪里 where?
nàme 那么 that, so
nán dào bù shì mā? 难道不是吗? a rhetorical "isn't it so?" [expects the answer "是"]
nǎo 脑 brain
ne 呢 [indicates sentence is a question]
nèi xīn 内心 inner heart
néng 能 to be able to
nǐ 你 you
nián 年 year
niánqīng 年轻 young
núlì 奴隶 slave
ōu'zhōu 欧洲 Europe
pèide 配得 worthy
pǐngé 品格 character
píngshí 平时 usually
pǐnzhì 品质 quality, character
pǔbiàn 普遍 common, commonly
qián 前 before, ago
qián 钱 money
qiǎohé 巧合 coincidence
qíguài 奇怪 strange
qīngchǔ 清楚 clear, clearly
qíngkuàng 情况 situation

qīnqíng 亲情 family
qīnrén 亲人 family member, relative
qīpiàn 欺骗 to cheat, to deceive
qǐshì 启示 revelation
qǐshì gěi 启示给 to reveal to [or "to give to by means of revelation"]
qíshí 其实 actually
qítā de 其他的 other
qǐyuán 起源 origin
qīzi 妻子 wife
quán 全 complete
qǔdé 取得 to achieve
quán shìjiè 全世界 the whole world
què 却 actually, in actuality
quēdiǎn 缺点 shortcoming
ràng 让 to allow, to compel
ránhòu 然后 after
rén 人 people
rènhé 任何 any
rènhé rén 任何人 anybody [literally "any person"]
rénkǒu 人口 population
rénlèi 人类 humanity, human being
rénshēng 人生 life
rènshì 认识 to meet, to know
rénxìng 人性 humanity
ròushēn 肉身 flesh, incarnate, "flesh-and-blood"
rúguǒ 如果 if
sèqíng 色情 pornography, pornographic
shǎo 少 few
shārén 杀人 murder, to murder
shāsǐ 杀死 to murder
shèhuì 社会 society, societal

shéi 谁 who?
shén 神 God
shēn 深 deep
shēn'ài 深爱 to love deeply
shēng xiǎohái 生小孩 to give birth to a child
shèngjí 圣洁 holy
shèngjīng 圣经 the Bible
shēnghuó 生活 life, livelyhood
shēngmìng 生命 life
shénme 什么 what
shēntǐ 身体 body
shēntǐ jiégōu 身体结构 anatomy
shénxìng 神性 divinity
shènzhì 甚至 even
shì 事 stuff [abstract, not physical]
shì...de 是[adjective]的 to be [adjective]
shìfǒu 是否 whether
shíhòu 时候 time
shìjiè 世界 the earth, the world
shìjiè shàng 世界上 on the earth
shìjièguān 世界观 worldview
shìqíng 事情 stuff [abstract, non-material], same as 事
shīwàng 失望 despair
shū 书 book
shú 赎 redemption
shújià 赎价 ransom
shùnxù 顺序 ordered, in succession
shuō 说 to speak
shuō de duì 说得对 to speak correctly
shuōhuà 说话 to speak, speech
shuōhuǎng 说谎 to lie, to tell a lie

shuōmíng　说明　directions, explanation, to explain
shúqīng　赎清　to redeem, to atone for [same as 赎]
sǐ　死　to die
sì bǎi　四百　four hundred
sǐlǐ　死里　death [literally "in death"]
sǐwáng　死亡　death
sòng gěi　送给　to give freely
sòng gěi wǒ de　送给我的　"freely given to me"
suíjī　随机　random
suīrán...dànshì　虽然...但是　even though...but
sùzhì　素质　quality (refers to the inner quality and character of a person)
suǒyǐ　所以　so
suǒyǒu　所有　all, every
tā　他　he
tā　它　it
tài...le　太[adjective]了　extremely [adjective], too [adjective]
tàidù　态度　attitude
tèbié　特别　especially, special
tì　替　on behalf of, for
tì...fù　替...付　to pay for [literally "for...to pay"]
tiāntáng　天堂　Heaven
tiáolǐ　条理　orderliness
tīng　听　to listen
tīngjiàn　听见　to hear
tōngguò　通过　by means of, through
tǒngyī　统一　unity, unified
tóngyì　同意　to agree
tōu　偷　to steal
túxiàng　图像　image

wǎngwǎng 往往 often
wánměi 完美 perfect
wánquán 完全 completely
wéi 为 for
wěidà 伟大 great, mighty
wéishénme 为什么 why
wénhuà 文化 culture
wèntí 问题 problem
wǒ 我 me, I
wǒmen 我们 we, us
wú 无 without
wú suǒ bù néng 无所不能 omnipotent [literally "nothing [God] cannot do"]
wú suǒ bù zhī 无所不知 all-knowing [literally "nothing [God] does not know"]
wú suǒ bù zài 无所不在 omnipresent [literally "nowhere [God] is not"]
wú zuì 无罪 sinless
wùlǐ 物理 physical, physics
wúshénlùn 无神论 Atheism
wùzhì 物质 physical, material
xiàlái 下来 down [usually used in reference to something moving down, being written down, etc.]
xiàng 向 to
xiǎng 想 to want
xiǎngfǎ 想法 thought, idea, view
xiāngxìn 相信 to believe, to have faith in
xiànzài 现在 now
xiě 写 to write
xiě gěi 写给 to write to [you can think of it as meaning "to give to by means of writing"]
xié'è 邪恶 evil

xiěxià de 写下的 written down
xīfāng 西方 the West
xīfāngrén 西方人 Westerners
xíguàn 习惯 habit
xǐhuān 喜欢 to like, to enjoy
xìn (1) 信 letter
xìn (2) 信 to believe
xīn 新 new
xíngwéi 行为 actions, behaviors
xīnlíng 心灵 soul
xīnlǐ 心里 in one's heart
xìnyǎng 信仰 faith
xīnyuē 新约 the New Testament
xīshēng 牺牲 sacrifice, to sacrifice
xīwàng 希望 hope, to hope
xuéxí 学习 to study
xūyào 需要 need, to need, to need to
yàng 样 kind, type
yàngshì 样式 style
yányǔ 言语 language
yāoqiú 要求 to require, requirement
yàzhōu 亚洲 Asia
yēsū 耶稣 Jesus
yě 也 also
yì 亿 one hundred million [so that means 20亿 is 2 billion]
yī běn rénshēng shuōmíng shū 一本人生说明书 "a life instruction-manual"
yī fēng xìn 一封信 a letter
yī gè...yě méi yǒu 一个[noun]也没有 to have not even one [noun]

yī kàn...jiù 一看[noun]就 as soon as one looks at [noun]
yībān 一般 usually
yīdìng 一定 certainly, certain
yǐhòu 以后 after, later
yǐjīng 已经 already
yīkào 依靠 to rely on
yīn wéi...suǒ yǐ 因为...所以 because...so
yīncǐ 因此 therefore
yīngdāng 应当 ought to, must, should
yíngdé 赢得 to earn
yǐngxiǎng 影响 influence, to influence
yīnyuè 音乐 music
yīqǐ 一起 together
yǐqián 以前 before, ago
yīrán 依然 still, as before
yìsī 意思 meaning
yīsīlánjiāo 伊斯兰教 Islam
yǐwéi 以为 to think erroneously
yīxiē 一些 a few
yīyàng 一样 the same, similar
yìyì 意义 meaning, significance
yīzhí 一直 continuously, always
yìzhì 意志 will [the noun, as in "God's will" or "your will be done"]
yīzhǒng 一种 a kind of, a type of
yòng 用 to use, to apply
yǒngyuǎn 永远 eternal
yǒu 有 to have
yǒu qián de rén 有钱的人 rich people
yǒu shíhòu 有时候 sometimes [literally "there are

times"]
yǒuqíng 友情 friendship, friend
yóutàirén 犹太人 Jewish people
yǔ 与 with
yǔ zhòu wàn wù 宇宙万物 universe [basically means the same as 宇宙]
yǔ...yǒu guān 与[noun]有关 having to do with [noun]
yuànyì 愿意 to be willing, to be willing to
yuántóu 源头 origin, source
yùbèi 预备 to prepare
yùndòng 运动 motion, movement
yùnzhuǎn 运转 operations, functioning
yǔzhòu 宇宙 universe
zài 在 at
zài...lǐ 在...里 in
zài yīqǐ 在一起 to be together
zànshí 暂时 temporary
zěnmeyàng 怎么样 how
zěnmebàn 怎么办 what to do?
zěnyàng 怎样 how
zhàngfū 丈夫 husband
zhǎodào 找到 to find
zhe 着 [used to indicate the preceding verb/action is ongoing]
zhě 者 one who does [preceding word]
zhège 这个 this
zhēnde 真的 really, actually
zhěng gè 整个 the whole, the entire
zhèngmíng 证明 proof, to prove
zhèngquè 正确 true, correct
zhèngshì 正式 formal, official

zhēnlǐ 真理 truth
zhēnzhèng 真正 actual, real
zhèxiē 这些 these
zhèyàng 这样 this kind of, this type of
zhǐ 只 just, only
zhīdào 知道 to know
zhīqián 之前 before
zhǒng 种 kind, type
zhōngdōng 中东 the Middle East
zhōngguó 中国 China
zhōngguórén 中国人 Chinese people
zhòngyào 重要 important
zhǔ 主 Lord
zhù 住 to live
zhuàn 赚 to earn
zhuānyè 专业 professional
zhùfú 祝福 blessed
zhújiàn 逐渐 gradually
zìjǐ 自己 by oneself
zìrán 自然 nature, natural
zìshā 自杀 suicide
zìxìn 自信 self-confidence
zōngjiào 宗教 religion, religious
zòngrán 纵然 despite
zǒu 走 to walk
zǒu zìjǐ de lù 走自己的路 "to walk one's own road"
zuì 最 [makes the following word/phrase a superlative]
zuì 罪 sin
zuì yǒu luójí 最有逻辑 having the most logic
zuì'è 罪恶 sin
zuì'è gǎn 罪恶感 guilt, guilty feeling

zūnchóng 尊崇 respected, honored
zūnzhào 遵照 in accordance with
zuò 做 to do

Made in the USA
Columbia, SC
18 December 2017